M000219490

ANTIDOTES
&
STEPPING
STONES

ANTIDOTES & STEPPING STONES

Powerful prescriptions for spiritual health
based on the spirituality
of St. Faustina

Rev. George W. Kosicki, C.S.B.
Foreword by Vinny Flynn

Spirit Song Ministries
Stockbridge, Massachusetts

Unless otherwise indicated, Scripture quotations
are from the New American Bible (NAB).

Quotations from the diary of St. Faustina are from the
official English language edition, *Divine Mercy in My Soul*,
© 1987 Congregation of Marians. Used by permission.
All rights reserved.

Image of Blessed M. Faustina Kowalska,
The Apostle of Mercy, by Janis Balabon, page 15.
© 1994 Marians of the Immaculate Conception;
printed with permission.

Image of The Divine Mercy by Robert Skemp, page 21.
© 1982 Marians of the Immaculate Conception,
Stockbridge, Massachusetts; all world rights reserved;
reprinted with permission.

Cover Photo: Paul Rocheleau
Fr. Kosicki photos: Vinny Flynn

Except for brief quotations in reviews or articles, no
part of this book may be reproduced, stored in a
retrieval system, or transmitted in any form or by any
means, electronic, mechanical, photocopying, or
otherwise, without the prior written permission of
the publisher.

Edited by Vinny Flynn
Book design by Dianne Cooper Bridges
Printed in the United States of America

Library of Congress Catalog Card No: 00-102528
ISBN 1-884479-13-8

Copyright © 2000 Rev. George W. Kosicki, C.S.B.
All rights reserved.

Published by Spirit Song Ministries
P.O. Box 486
Stockbridge, MA 01262

THANKS . . .

To Vinny Flynn for the inspiration and challenge to write on the spirituality of St. Faustina.

To Father Ed Sylvia, C.S.C. and my brother Witold for their helpful suggestions on the description of the human condition.

To Christine Kruszyna for her patient perseverance in preparing the manuscript.

To Sister Mary Ann Follmar for her encouragement and support.

"Not even the fangs
of poisonous reptiles
overcame your sons,
for your mercy
brought the antidote
to heal them."

Wisdom 16:10

"Jesus has a remedy for everything."

St. Faustina
Diary, 447

CONTENTS

FOREWORD

Antidotes and Stepping Stones offers specific remedies for the unavoidable stress and suffering that fill our lives and for the unhealthy tendencies and attitudes that so often plague us, spreading through our systems like poison.

Fr. Kosicki identifies twelve common human ailments — twelve "poisons" that can weaken and even destroy us in mind, body, heart, and soul.

For each of these ailments, he prescribes an antidote, drawn from the spirituality of St. Faustina. So, for the poison we call "Fear," for example, the antidote from Faustina is "Trust."

Each of the twelve antidotes is reinforced by scripture passages and by excerpts from the diary of St. Faustina. Fr. Kosicki also adds his own insights, showing how the antidotes can be used not only as ways to counteract the negative content of our lives but also as stepping stones that lead us to sanctity.

Please, don't just read this book. Use it to discover where you need God's healing touch, from day to day, and take regular doses of the medicine you need.

Vinny Flynn

HOW TO USE THIS BOOK

This is a "How to" book. It shows how to respond to your day-by-day human condition and how to become an Apostle of Mercy like St. Faustina.

Each day may find you in a different situation or mood which calls for a different way of responding. This book can be a companion to help you discern, by the light of the Holy Spirit, the most fruitful response to the present moment.

The antidotes presented here can be taken as pills every time we need them, or like time-release capsules to provide continuing protection. The antidotes build up our spiritual immune systems and shield us from the onslaught of human weakness and sin.

Each of the antidotes is a decision, an act of the will, to do something or not to do something. At times it is a prayer, a short phrase we repeat over and over again from the heart. At other times it is an invitation to the Lord, or a permission we give to Him so that He can freely act. Or it may be a silent presence of heart to the Lord who is present in our hearts ... a decision to unite our hearts with His ... a moment of loving union with the Lord who loves us and is present to us by His Holy Spirit. It is always an act of mercy by deed, word, or prayer (*Diary*, 742).

In various situations and times we may well use more than one antidote at a time. It is not unusual to move from one to another as we respond to our varying human situations, and yet, we have all experienced special moments of such darkness and weakness that we need all twelve antidotes at the same time! All the antidotes are available to us at any time and in any situation. They are gifts given to us to be used!

As we use these twelve antidotes to counteract our human misery, they become stepping stones that lead us across the mire of our human condition to spiritual growth, maturity, and interior peace. They transform us, step by step, into apostles of God's mercy — into living Eucharist — so that we may radiate His mercy by the witness of our lives.

These antidotes were gleaned from the diary of St. Faustina, *Divine Mercy in My Soul*, and they summarize her spiritual life.

But they are not unique to St. Faustina; rather, they are fundamental to a life lived in union with Christ, and many Christians have been transformed by them. St. Faustina is unique, however, in her special union with Christ as the secretary of Divine Mercy. Recording everything the Lord taught her, along with her own responses to these teachings, she describes not only the moments of ecstatic grace, but also the dark and miserable moments.

Thanks be to God for this record of the human condition and her response to it, because it helps us to identify with her in our struggle for spiritual growth. Her honest record of how she used the antidotes as strong medicine against negative attitudes and situations and as stepping stones to sanctity is an inspiration and challenge to all of us who want to be transformed into apostles of Divine Mercy.

A NEW SAINT FOR A NEW MILLENNIUM. On Mercy Sunday, April 30, 2000, Sister Maria Faustina of the Most Blessed Sacrament became the first saint of the Jubilee Year ushering in the Third Millennium. Known as the Apostle of Divine Mercy, she deeply understood the merciful Heart of Jesus and knew that she was to be an instrument of His healing love. He had told her:

> I do not want to punish aching mankind, but I desire to heal it (Diary, 1588). On the day of My feast, the Feast of Mercy, you will go through the world and bring fainting souls to the spring of My mercy. I shall heal and strengthen them (Diary, 206).

FEAR

Being anxious, worried, afraid of death, the future, the unknown, sickness, violence, people.

TRUST

Having a living faith in Jesus, knowing that He is in charge, and that He loves us.

CHAPTER ONE

SCRIPTURAL RESPONSE:

Fear is useless, what is needed is trust (Mk 5:36).

It is I. Do not be afraid! (Mt 14:27).

Perfect love casts out all fear (1 Jn 4:18).

RESPONSE FROM ST. FAUSTINA:

The graces of My mercy are drawn by means of one vessel only, and that is trust. The more a soul trusts, the more it will receive. Souls that trust boundlessly are a great comfort to me. ... I pour all the treasures of my graces into them (*Diary*, 1578).

Mankind will not have peace until it turns with trust to My mercy (*Diary*, 300).

When my soul is in anguish, I think only in this way: Jesus is good and full of mercy, and even if the ground were to give way under my feet, I would not cease to trust in Him (*Diary*, 1192).

TRUST AS A STEPPING STONE TO SANCTITY

Trust is a living faith in the Lord, faith that He is, indeed, Lord, that He is in charge, and that He loves us with an infinite merciful love.

Trust gives God permission to act freely, so He can have mercy on all (see Rom 11:32). Lack of trust is the greatest obstacle to God acting, and it is what pains Him the most. Souls do not trust Him and so do not receive His mercy.

Our Lord told St. Faustina that "**the greatest sinners would achieve great sanctity, if only they would trust in My mercy**" (1784). "If only" is the key. If only souls would trust, they would overcome the obstacles of the human condition and take steps to grow spiritually.

The greatest obstacle of our human condition is *fear*. Fear paralyzes us and keeps us in bondage. The list of the fears and anxieties that plague us would fill a book! Yet Our Lord said in the gospel: "Fear is useless, what is needed is trust" (Mk 5:36).

How do we trust in the midst of fears? How do we use trust as an antidote to our fears and as a stepping stone to sanctity? What can you and I do?

We can repeat over and over again, from the heart, "Jesus, I trust in You!" That says it all. It is our way of living as Christians; it is our response to Jesus who is Mercy Itself, who stands at the door of our hearts waiting for us to open them even a little bit (see Rev 3:20 and *Diary*, 1486, 1507).

"Jesus, I trust in You!" is the response Jesus asks of us in return for His blessing of merciful love. He asked that the image of Himself as the Merciful Savior be signed "Jesus, I trust in you!" This image of Jesus is a vessel with which we "gather" mercy; it is a reminder to trust in Him.

So how can you grow in TRUST? Gaze upon the image of the Merciful Savior often; carry it with you, place it in your home and office, and even on the dashboard of your car — and cry out from your hearts each time you look at it: "Jesus, I trust in You!"

Place all your fears into His Merciful Heart and trust. Open the doors of your heart and TRUST Jesus!

In the midst of the battle cry shout the victory cheer: T.R.U.S.T.!

Total
Reliance
Upon
Saving
Truth

"If you continue in my word ... you will know the truth, and the truth will make you free. ... If the Son makes you free, you will be free indeed" (Jn 8:31-36, RSV).

JESUS I TRUST IN YOU

"Anyone can ... look at this image of the merciful Jesus, His Heart radiating grace, and hear in the depths of his own soul what Blessed Faustina heard: 'Fear nothing. I am with you always' (Diary, 586). And if this person responds with a sincere heart, 'Jesus, I trust in You,' he will find comfort in all his anxieties and fears."

— Pope John Paul II

SHAME

Feeling inadequate, unworthy,
unlovable, sinful, dirty, burdened by
past sins and failures.

MERCY

Turning to God's mercy,
accepting it, being transformed by it,
and letting it flow out to others.

CHAPTER TWO

SCRIPTURAL RESPONSE:

We must celebrate and rejoice, because your brother was dead and has come to life again (Lk 15:32, NABR).

Be merciful even as your Father is merciful (Lk 6:36, RSV).

Blessed are the merciful for they shall obtain mercy (Mt 5:7, RSV).

RESPONSE FROM ST. FAUSTINA:

I am mercy itself (*Diary*, 1739; see also 281, 300, 1074, 1148, 1273, 1777).

I understood that the greatest attribute is love and mercy. It unites the creature with the Creator. This immense love and abyss of mercy are made known in the Incarnation of the Word and in the Redemption [of humanity], and it is here that I saw this as the greatest of all God's attributes (*Diary*, 180).

I am giving you three ways of exercising mercy toward your neighbor: the first — by deed, the second — by word, the third — by prayer (*Diary*, 742).

My mercy is greater than your sins and those of the entire world (*Diary*, 1485).

MERCY AS A STEPPING STONE TO SANCTITY

Mercy is God's love poured out upon us miserable sinners, love poured through His pierced Heart as a fount of mercy for us. It is love's second name (John Paul II, *Rich in Mercy*).

A victory cheer capsulizes mercy as God Himself:

Mighty
Eternal
Redeeming
Compassionate
Yahweh

Our Lord taught St. Faustina that He is mercy itself, that His mercy is like a vast, bottomless ocean. It is greater than all our sins, all our fears, all our anxieties, all our darkness and depression; and it is available for everyone.

> **Urge all souls to trust in the unfathomable abyss of My mercy, because I want to save them all. On the cross, the fountain of My mercy was opened wide by the lance for all souls — no one have I excluded!** (1182)

> **Write that I am more generous toward sinners than toward the just** (1275).

God's mercy is always available. His plan and His desire is to have mercy on all (see Rom 11:32). He wants no one to escape His mercy. But, because of our free will, we can frustrate His plan by not accepting His mercy.

One of the greatest obstacles to accepting His mercy is our *shame*. Because of our past sins and failures we feel unlovable, unworthy, dirty, miserable, distressed, distrustful, anxious, and tormented. Shame is the response of Adam and Eve to their sin. Shame is the most common response of those who have sinned and turned away from God's mercy.

And yet there is something worse than our shame and sin — not turning to the mercy of God after we have sinned. The Lord waits for us to turn to Him, just as the father waits for his prodigal son (Lk 15:11-32). By His mercy, the Lord wants to restore our dignity, our worth, and our value. This is cause for rejoicing! (John Paul II, *Rich in Mercy*, 5-6).

The antidote to shame is *Mercy* — God's Divine Mercy. This antidote becomes a stepping stone to transformation and sanctity as we turn to His mercy, accept it, let it transform us, and let it flow out to others.

The Lord commands us to use His mercy, to be merciful even as our heavenly Father is merciful (see Lk 6:36). We are to be merciful to others by deed, word, and prayer (see *Diary*, 742). As we are merciful to others, we, ourselves, obtain more mercy: "Blessed are the merciful for they shall obtain mercy" (Mt 5:7, RSV); and at the same time we are merciful to the Lord Himself (see Mt 25:40 and *Rich in Mercy*, 8).

How can I be merciful in a practical way? By humbly doing the Corporal and Spiritual Works of Mercy.

The Corporal Works of Mercy are feeding the hungry, giving drink to the thirsty, clothing the naked, sheltering the travelers, comforting the prisoners, visiting the sick, and burying the dead.

The Spiritual Works of Mercy include teaching the ignorant, praying for the living and the dead, correcting the sinners, counseling those in doubt, consoling the sorrowful, bearing wrongs patiently, and forgiving wrongs willingly.

The following prayer for mercy is always a practical and effective way to receive and use God's mercy as a stepping stone toward transformation and sanctity:

> Jesus, fill me with your mercy, that I may be merciful, that I may radiate your mercy. Jesus, Mercy!

The prayer "Jesus, Mercy!" is not only a plea for mercy on us and on the whole world; it is also a cry of praise and thanksgiving for Jesus, who is Mercy Itself. This prayer should arise from our hearts as a continuous plea for mercy, especially as we see the shame, sin, and misery in our own lives and in the lives of all in the world.

REBELLION

Being angry, full of hatred,
unwilling, judgmental,
unforgiving, aggressive.

GOD'S WILL

Seeking to live in joyful
acceptance of God's will, desiring
His will above all else.

CHAPTER THREE

SCRIPTURAL RESPONSE:

Your will be done (Mt 6:10; 26:42).

I have come to do your will (Heb 10:9).

Not everyone who says to me, 'Lord, Lord,' will enter the kingdom of heaven, but only the one who does the will of my Father (Mt 7:21).

RESPONSE FROM ST. FAUSTINA:

The Lord Jesus gave me to know how very pleasing to Him is a soul who lives in accordance with the will of God. It thereby gives very great glory to God (*Diary* 821; see also 724, 952).

There is one word I heed and continually ponder; it alone is everything to me; I live by it and die by it, and it is the holy will of God. It is my daily food. My whole soul listens intently to God's wishes. I do always what God asks of me, although my nature often quakes and I feel the magnitude of these things is beyond my strength. I know well what I am of myself, but I also know what the grace of God is, which supports me (*Diary* 652).

GOD'S WILL AS A STEPPING STONE TO SANCTITY

"Your will be done!" is the prayer that Jesus taught us (Mt 6:10) and the prayer that He lived: "Take this cup away from me, but not what I will but what you will" (Mk 14:36, NABR). Jesus came to do the will of His Father (see Heb 10:9): "My food is to do the will of the one who sent me and to finish his work" (Jn 4:34, NABR).

Mary, Our Blessed Mother, expressed this submission to the will of God at the Annunciation: "Let it be done to me according to your word" (Lk 1:38, NABR). St. Paul expressed his submission by saying: "It is no longer I who live but Christ, who lives in me" (Gal 2:20, RSV).

St. Faustina was instructed by Our Lord to cross out her own will in a graphic way:

> **Write these words on a clean sheet of paper: 'From today on, my own will does not exist,' and then cross out the page. And on the other side write these words: 'From today on, I do the Will of God everywhere, always, and in everything'** (372).

The contact point of God's will and our will is the point of interaction of God's freedom and our freedom. God's glory is that He created us free and He will not violate that freedom. He asks, invites, encourages, cajoles, knocks, and waits for us to act freely in submitting to His will, where we find real freedom. This is the very paradox of the gospel — in dying we are born to eternal life. When we die to our self-will, we find eternal life in His will.

What is the result when we focus on our own will? Rebellion! A rebellious attitude that echoes the cry of Lucifer, "I will not serve!" A rebellion that expresses itself in anger, hatred, cursing, self-righteous judgments and questioning, self-reliance, and self-determination. This rebellion is the root of all sin.

And what is the antidote to our rebellious spirit? God's will. As we seek God's will and actually do it, we take steps to transformation and sanctity. The basic issue is: "Your will be done." There are two parts to it: first, that it be God's will and not just mine or others'; and secondly, that it actually be done according to His plan and timing.

But then comes the important question: "What is God's will?" What does God want for me, moment by moment, in my daily living?

- He wants us all to be saved and come to the knowledge of the truth (1 Tm 2:4).
- He wants to have mercy on all (Rom 11:32).
- He wants to establish His Kingdom in our hearts by the Holy Spirit (see Mt 6:10; Rom 5:5).
- He wants us to obey His commandments (Mt 19:16-26).
- He wants us to be merciful even as He is merciful (Lk 6:36).
- He wants us to love one another as He loves us (Jn 13:34).

- He wants us to eat His flesh and drink His blood and have eternal life (Jn 6:54).
- He wants us to obey His Church (Mt 16:19; Jn 20:23).
- He wants us to live as members of His family (Col 3:12-20).
- He wants us to call Him "Our Father," "Abba" (Mt 6:9; Jn 20:17).
- He wants to give us His Holy Spirit (Lk 10:13; 24:49; Acts 1:8).
- He wants us to take Mary as Our Mother (Jn 19:26-27).
- He wants us to learn to be gentle and humble of heart (Mt 11:28-29).

God's will is expressed throughout Sacred Scripture. One especially beautiful expression of it is found in the writings of St. Paul, who gives us a practical way of doing God's will moment by moment, using this antidote as a stepping stone to growth:

> Rejoice always.
> Pray without ceasing.
> In all things give thanks, for this is the will
> of God in Christ Jesus regarding you all
> (1 Thess 5:16-18, Confraternity Edition).

"This is the will of God ... regarding *you all*." It is in the plural; it is the will of God for everybody, and at all times, and it is always available for us. In this way we can surrender our wills to His will, His plans, and His pleasure.

But what if I don't know God's will in a particular

From today on,
my own will
does not exist.

From today on,
I do the Will of God
everywhere, always,
and in everything.

situation? I can still surrender my will to His by asking for light to see His will, and by praying for the strength to follow that will. When we use our free will to surrender to the will of God, He will certainly bless our decision by revealing that will to us.

Our battle cry in life, our antidote to our rebellious spirit, and our stepping stone to sanctity is: "Father, your will be done!"

SELFISHNESS

Being self-centered, self-concerned,
self-seeking, self-fulfilling,
pleasure seeking.

GLORIFYING
GOD'S MERCY

Focusing on God instead
of on ourselves, praising and
proclaiming His mercy.

CHAPTER FOUR

SCRIPTURAL RESPONSE:

Go home to your family and make it clear to them how much the Lord in His mercy has done for you (Mk 5:19-20).

I will give thanks to you among the peoples, O Lord; I will chant your praise among the nations, for your kindness towers to the heavens, and your faithfulness to the skies (Ps 108).

RESPONSE FROM ST. FAUSTINA:

Give praise and glory to this mercy of Mine (*Diary*, 206).

By this means [mercy toward others by deed, word and prayer] a soul glorifies and pays reverence to My mercy (*Diary*, 742).

I expect from you, My child, a great number of souls who will glorify My mercy for all eternity (*Diary*, 1489).

I demand ... that people revere My mercy (*Diary*, 742).

GLORIFYING GOD'S MERCY AS A STEPPING STONE TO SANCTITY

To glorify God's mercy is to reverence it and acknowledge it as His greatest attribute (John Paul II, *Rich in Mercy* 14; *Diary*, 180). Glorifying the mercy of God was the very reason and purpose of St. Faustina's life: "Glorifying Your mercy," she wrote, "is the exclusive task of my life" (*Diary*, 1242). She glorified God's mercy in all her words, deeds, and prayers.

Glorifying God's mercy can be defined by a series of words that begin with the letter "p": praising it; praying for it; pleading for it; proclaiming it; and, especially, practicing mercy to others.

After his healing of the demoniac, Jesus shows that He wants His mercy glorified, telling him to return to his home and tell his family about God's mercy to him. (Mk 5:19-20). To glorify God's mercy is to tell others what God has done for you, to tell your family, your friends, anyone who will listen to you.

We should all tell others about God's desire to pour out His mercy especially on sinners and on the miserable (*Diary*, 723, 1275). We should tell them that His mercy is greater than all our sin and misery (*Diary*, 699).

Like St. Faustina, who was conscious of her mission in the church to constantly plead for mercy (see *Diary*, 482), we, too, can plead for mercy on the whole church and world, and so glorify His mercy.

Like St. Faustina, we can write about His mercy or distribute leaflets about Divine Mercy.

We can also support with prayer and with funds those who are glorifying God's mercy by writing and preaching. Pray especially for their strength and protection because they are in the front lines of this spiritual warfare. Like St. Faustina, they know how Satan hates God's mercy (*Diary*, 412, 520, 1496-1499).

Our Lord gave St. Faustina great promises for those who glorify His mercy:

> **All those souls who will glorify My mercy and spread its worship, encouraging others to trust in My mercy, will not experience terror at the hour of death (1540).**

> **With those that glorify and proclaim My great mercy to others, I will deal according to My infinite mercy at the hour of their death (379).**

> **In this book [of life] are written the names of the souls that have glorified My mercy (689).**

Glorifying God's mercy is the *antidote* to our human condition of *selfishness*. Turning to God's mercy overcomes our self-seeking, self-concern, self-fulfillment, and pleasure seeking.

When we glorify God's mercy, we focus our lives on Him, instead of ourselves, as number one. We then realize that God is God and we are not. When we turn to Him in our human condition, He can transform us into holy vessels of His great mercy.

Glorifying God's mercy is the precious golden door by

which we enter into union with Him. It is the great response of the Blessed Mother in her Magnificat:

> "My soul proclaims the greatness of the Lord; my spirit rejoices in God my Savior. ... The Mighty One has done great things for me, and holy is His name. ... His mercy is from age to age" (Lk 1:46-50).

SECULARIZATION

Living as though there
were no God, or being indifferent
to God (practical atheism).

GLORIFYING
THE TRINITY

Living as children of God,
rejoicing in the Three Divine persons
living in our hearts.

CHAPTER FIVE

SCRIPTURAL RESPONSE:

The proof that you are sons is the fact that God has sent forth into our hearts the Spirit of His Son which cries out 'Abba!' ('Father!') (Gal 4:6).

Whoever loves me will keep my word, and my Father will love him, and we will come to him and make our dwelling with him. ... The Advocate, the Holy Spirit that the Father will send in my name — He will teach you everything and remind you of all that I told you (Jn 14:23-26).

RESPONSE FROM ST. FAUSTINA:

I was drawn into the bosom of the Most Holy Trinity (*Diary*, 1670).

Jesus, when you come to me in Holy Communion, You who together with the Father and the Holy Spirit have deigned to dwell in the little heaven of my heart, I try to keep you company throughout the day (*Diary*, 486).

GLORIFYING THE TRINITY AS A STEPPING STONE TO SANCTITY

The most obvious impression upon reading the *Diary* of St. Faustina, even a part of it, is that she lived in an intimate communion with God. She saw Him, talked to Him, listened to Him, suffered with Him, and loved Him with her whole heart, mind and strength. God was all to her.

The message of her life is clear: God exists, He is real, He is present, He loves us, and He wants us to be united with Him.

In our human condition we so easily live as though God doesn't exist. It is a form of practical atheism. At least the real atheist has the politeness to deny God. But in our age so many live in indifference to Him. They glorify themselves in a parody of the Gloria: "Glory to man in the highest, and peace to the man with the most!"

The antidote to this secularization, to this forgetfulness of God, is to glorify Him — Father, Son, and Holy Spirit. We glorify God when we respond to the fact that He exists, that He is love, and that He wants to transform us in a loving union with Him. We respond to Him by praise, worship, thanksgiving, and love — a love of Him with our whole heart, mind, and strength, and a love of one another.

We glorify the Holy Trinity when we accept the love of the Father and the Son, poured into our hearts by the Holy Spirit (see Rom 5:5). The Father creating us, the Son redeeming us, and the Holy Spirit sanctifying us — all are gifts of mercy.

As we receive these gifts of mercy, we learn to live in an intimate relationship with each person of the Trinity. St. Faustina writes:

> Once after Holy Communion, I heard these words: You are our dwelling place. At that moment, I felt in my soul the presence of the Holy Trinity: the Father, the Son, and the Holy Spirit (*Diary*, 451).

And again, during a time of Eucharistic adoration:

> I knew more distinctly than ever before the Three Divine Persons, the Father, the Son, and the Holy Spirit. My soul is in communion with these Three. ... Whoever is united to One of the Three Persons is thereby united to the whole Blessed Trinity, for this Oneness is indivisible (*Diary*, 472).

What should our response be for this wonderful gift? St. Faustina explains that we should glorify the Trinity by loving as God loves:

> The Holy Trinity grants me Its life abundantly, by the gift of the Holy Spirit. The Three Divine Persons live in me. When God loves, He loves with all His Being, with all the power of His Being. If God has loved me in this way, how should I respond — I, His spouse (392)?

St. Faustina, from her experience of being drawn up into the bosom of the Most Holy Trinity and being immersed in the pure love of God (see *Diary*, 1121, 1129, 1670), teaches us how to use this antidote of glorifying the Holy Trinity as a stepping stone to sanctity:

> Today, I live, glorifying the Holy Trinity. I thank God that he has deigned to adopt us as His children, through grace (1819).
>
> O my Jesus, how very easy it is to become holy; all that is needed is a bit of good will. ... Faithfulness to the inspirations of the Holy Spirit — that is the shortest route (291).

MISERY

Being sick, in pain,
inept, unable, worried, anxious,
gloomy, dissipated, sinful.

SUFFERING
FOR OTHERS

Offering our here-and-now
sufferings and pain for others
in union with Jesus.

SCRIPTURAL RESPONSE:

I rejoice in my sufferings for your sake, and in my flesh I complete what is lacking in Christ's afflictions for the sake of His body; that is, the Church (Col 1:24, RSV).

RESPONSE FROM ST. FAUSTINA:

I desire that you make an offering of yourself for sinners and especially for those souls who have lost hope in God's mercy (*Diary*, 308).

Mother of God, Your soul was plunged into a sea of bitterness; look upon Your child and teach her to suffer and to love while suffering (*Diary*, 315).

I am giving you a share in the redemption of mankind (*Diary*, 310).

Oh, if only the suffering soul knew how it is loved by God, it would die of joy and excess of happiness! Some day, we will know the value of suffering, but then we will no longer be able to suffer. The present moment is ours (*Diary*, 963).

SUFFERING FOR SOULS AS A STEPPING STONE TO SANCTITY

The most obvious condition of mankind, the one that is common to all of us, is misery and suffering. We all have pain. None of us can escape it; it seems to be always with us. So what can we do about it? Our present society tells us to escape from it. Suffering and pain are to be eliminated as quickly as possible: seek out a pill, a doctor, a vacation, a pleasure that will distract you from the pain. The message is that pain is useless and without meaning.

The presence of suffering in the world is probably the greatest excuse for denying God. How can there be a merciful God who allows suffering? How can there be a God who wants innocent children to suffer? And the list of complaints goes on.

But, there is another side to suffering. Suffering was the way God the Father chose for His Son Jesus to show us ultimate love and mercy, and ultimate humility. By His love, Jesus transformed suffering to bring salvation to all mankind. By His suffering, He Himself was "perfected ... designated as high priest ..." (see Heb 5:9-10 and Pope John Paul II, *The Christian Meaning of Human Suffering*, Feb. 11, 1984).

Then, Jesus extended His invitation to us to share in the work of redemption, to be partners with Him by offering our sufferings with love, united with Him as members of His Body: "All this is as God intends, for it is your special privilege to take Christ's part — not only to believe in Him but also to suffer for Him" (Phil 1:29).

How beautifully Pope John Paul II invited the over five hundred sick on stretchers in St. Peter's Basilica to offer their sufferings for the church leaders (Feb. 11, 1984). The Holy Father went on to point out that Jesus taught us two things about suffering: one, to do good to those who suffer; and two, to do good *with* the suffering.

St. Paul could find his joy in the suffering he endured for our sake as he filled up in his own flesh what was lacking in the sufferings of Christ (see Col 1:24). How could Paul find joy in his suffering? Because he found *meaning* in suffering. It brings mercy and salvation to others (see John Paul II, Feb 11, 1984).

What was lacking in the sufferings of Christ? He had not yet suffered in Paul, in you, and in me — He wanted to show the fullness of love and give us an opportunity to show love and share in the work of redemption. What a *mystery*! Christ lives and suffers in you and me: "The mystery of Christ in you, the hope of glory" (Col 1:27).

The *key* to suffering is suffering for *others*, for souls. When we offer our present, here-and-now sufferings and pain for others, with love, united with Jesus, especially in the Eucharist, we do a meaningful, precious, and effective work of intercession and redemption. We bring God's mercy and salvation to souls in need. By our suffering for souls, we bring to them the mercy and salvation won for us on the cross by Jesus. We are ambassadors of Christ, bringing His reconciliation (see 2 Cor 5:20).

Suffering for souls is not masochism. We do not seek suffering for the sake of suffering itself but rather for the sake of others. We do not need to take on extra sufferings. There are plenty for all of us in our daily life! As a special grace, the Lord calls certain privileged souls to a more intensive suffering for souls, as He called St. Faustina. This grace must be responded to only under the direction of a spiritual director, and in humility.

Suffering for souls does not mean we neglect our health. We are to be good stewards of the bodies the Lord has given us and take normal care for our physical, emotional, and spiritual health. Care for our health makes it possible for us to work effectively for the Kingdom of God and salvation of souls.

How do we offer up our sufferings? What do we actually do? We make an act of the will and say with our heart, "Lord Jesus I offer you this pain, this misery, this suffering for souls. I offer it in union with your passion, death, and resurrection offered at each Holy Mass."

Various ways can be used to express the offering. The point is to lovingly unite our suffering with the suffering of Christ — for souls. We can direct our offering to specific souls if we wish, naming the person(s) of our concern. The words are not essential; what is essential is the intention to offer our sufferings with Jesus for others.

Jesus, for souls.
Jesus, with you in your passion.
Jesus, accept my pain for souls.
Jesus, I offer this _____ in love.

The offering of our suffering and pain will not take away the pain, but it will give it meaning and value. "How do we suffer?" asks Pope John Paul II. Then he answers his own question, "With great pain!" (Feb 11, 1984).

St. Peter writes: "There is cause for rejoicing here. You may for a time have to suffer the distress of many trials, but this is so that your faith, which is more precious than fire-tried gold, may by its genuineness lead to praise, glory, and honor when Jesus Christ appears" (1 Peter 1:6-7).

St. Faustina learned the lesson of suffering for others from Our Lord. He asked her to make an offering of herself, uniting herself with His passion for the salvation of souls, especially sinners (see *Diary*, 135, 136, 137, 138, 186, 187, 190, 205, 206, 308, 309, 726). He wanted St. Faustina to be transformed by love:

> **I desire that you be entirely transformed into love and that you burn ardently as a pure victim of love** (726).

So, with complete obedience and faith, St. Faustina embraced suffering and came to know its value:

> Suffering is a great grace; through suffering the soul becomes like the Savior; in suffering, love becomes crystallized; the greater the suffering, the purer the love. (57)

Our Lord revealed to her the great mystery of suffering, telling her, "**I have need of your sufferings to rescue souls**" (1612).

God needs our sufferings!? Yes, God needs to continue His merciful outpouring of love through you and me. It seems that the love that Christ poured out on the world was not enough to show the depth and riches of His mercy; He wants to show that merciful love for souls through you and me! "It is your privilege to suffer for Christ" (Phil 1:29).

We can find our joy in that suffering for souls, just as St. Paul (Col 1:24) and St. Faustina did; "From the moment I came to love suffering," Faustina explains, "it ceased to be a suffering for me. Suffering is the daily food of my soul" (276). She even says that suffering can be "a delight," but only when love lends value to it (303, 351). Only *love* makes suffering valuable, precious, and a joy. What a mystery of love the Lord invites us to share!

Suffering for souls is the antidote to the human condition of misery. Suffering with love for souls, suffering with Christ, and allowing Christ to suffer in you, is the stepping stone to transformation and sanctity.

Suffering is precious! Don't waste it. Offer it! — with love, with and in Christ, for souls. This is our privilege: to take Christ's part, to bring His mercy to souls.

PRIDE

**Being self-righteous,
self-centered, rebellious,
judgmental, resentful, boastful.**

HUMILITY

**Realizing that God is God
and I am not. Being willing to serve
in humble, hidden ways.**

CHAPTER SEVEN

SCRIPTURAL RESPONSE:

Learn from me for I am gentle and humble of heart" (Mt 11:29).

He has cast down the mighty from their thrones, and has lifted up the lowly" (Lk 1:52, ICEL).

RESPONSE FROM ST. FAUSTINA:

Now I understand why there are so few saints; it is because so few souls are deeply humble (*Diary*, 1306).

Humiliation is my daily food (*Diary*, 92).

Nothing is better for the soul than humiliations. ... If there is a truly happy soul upon earth, it can only be a truly humble soul. ... A humble soul does not trust itself, but places all its confidence in God (*Diary*, 593).

HUMILITY AS A STEPPING STONE TO SANCTITY

Humility is not a popular virtue in our day. In fact, it's probably the most despised and ridiculed of virtues because it cuts to the heart of our human condition — *pride*. As sinful human beings, we are proud — self-righteous, self-centered, rebellious, resentful, and judgmental. Humility is the countersign to our proud age.

Because humility is the antidote to pride, it is the fundamental virtue of the spiritual life. Without humility there is no spiritual life. Jesus took the way of humility to reveal the Father's mercy and bring us salvation. As St. Paul expresses it, "He humbled himself, obediently accepting death, death on a cross! Because of this, God highly exalted him" (Phil 2:8-9).

St. Augustine, one of the great doctors of the Church, considered humility the way to sanctity:

> I would wish that you place yourself with all your love under Christ, and that you pave no other way in order to reach and to attain the truth than has already been paved by Him who, as God, knows the weakness of our steps. This way is, in the first place, humility; in the second place, humility; in the third place, humility. ... As often as you ask me about the Christian religion's norms of conduct, I choose to give no other answer than: humility (Letter 118, 2, 11).

In our own century, our Blessed Mother echoed St. Augustine as she taught St. Faustina about virtue:

> *I desire, My dearly beloved daughter, that you practice the three virtues that are dearest to Me — and most pleasing to God. The first is humility, humility and once again humility* (1415).

What is humility? First of all, it is the realization that God is God and I am not!

One key to humility is "**total gift**" — a gift of self and a gift of service. "God so loved the world that he *gave* his only Son" (Jn 3:16). God totally gave his Son as a sacrificial gift of love on the cross for us. Jesus expressed his humility in that He came "not to be served by others, but to *serve*, to *give* his own life as a ransom for the many" (Mt 20:28).

Another key to humility is "**other**." God is "other," and we love and serve Him; our neighbor is "other," and we love and serve him (or her). Humble, hidden, silent service is one of the great ways of expressing our humility — doing the simple tasks appropriate to our state of life; not blowing a trumpet to announce our great contribution, but doing the little things that no one else will see.

A third key to humility is "**transparency**." We are transparent when others see in us the Lord at work, when they see His mercy radiate from us, so that they are moved to give thanks to God. Transparency is characteristic of Jesus (When we look at Jesus we see the Father — see Jn 14:9); and of Mary (She leads us to Jesus: "Do whatever he tells you" — Jn 2:5). With Mary, we can live the Magnificat, giving constant praise and thanks to God for the great things He has done for the humble (see Lk 1:46-55).

Only the humble can receive God's mercy. Only the emptied can be filled. Only in dying are we born to eternal life. Humility is the necessary condition for spiritual growth. How beautifully Jesus, who is truth itself, calls us to learn humility from Him:

> Learn from me, for I am meek and *humble of heart*; and you will find rest for yourselves (Mt 11:29, NABR).

Humility is the most needed antidote for sinful humanity, and it is the cornerstone of sanctity.

SPIRITUAL WEAKNESS

Feeling fatigued,
depressed, burdened, bored,
lustful, intemperate, avaricious.

EUCHARIST

Taking time for "Radiation Therapy"
before the Eucharist, allowing God to
strengthen and transform us.

CHAPTER EIGHT

SCRIPTURAL RESPONSE:

He who feeds on my flesh and drinks my blood has life eternal (Jn 6:54).

RESPONSE FROM ST. FAUSTINA:

O Blessed Host, in whom is contained the medicine for all our infirmities (*Diary*, 356).

The most solemn moment of my life is the moment when I receive Holy Communion ... and for every Holy Communion I give thanks to the Most Holy Trinity (*Diary*, 1804).

Here is the tabernacle of Your mercy. Here is the remedy for all our ills (*Diary*, 1747).

All the good that is in me is due to Holy Communion. I owe everything to it. I feel that this holy fire has transformed me completely (*Diary*, 1392).

EUCHARIST AS A STEPPING STONE TO SANCTITY

"Taking bread and giving thanks, he broke it and gave it to them, saying: 'This is my body to be given for you. Do this as a remembrance of me.' Then He did the same with the cup after eating, saying as he did so: 'This cup is the new covenant in my blood, which will be shed for you'" (Lk 22:19-20).

The Eucharist is truly a miracle of mercy and of humility! God empties Himself in a total gift of merciful love, so that we may be filled with His life: "Just as the Father who has life sent me and I have life because of the Father, so the man who feeds on me will have life because of me" (Jn 6:57).

Because of the Eucharist we are transformed. We become what we eat — the living Body of the Lord. The Eucharist is the agent of transformation from a merely human life to a mature life as members of the mystical Body of Christ. Eucharist brings to fullness the seed of life given to us in Baptism (Vat II, P.O. #5).

St. Faustina, whose full religious name is Sister Maria Faustina of the Most Blessed Sacrament, prayed for this transformation:

> Jesus, transform me, miserable and sinful as I am, into Your own self (for You can do all things), and give me to Your Eternal Father. I want to become a sacrificial host before You, but an ordinary wafer to people (483).

St. Faustina was so transformed by the Holy Eucharist and by her total and humble giving of herself that Our Lord said to her: "**You are a living host, pleasing to the Heavenly Father**" (1826).

The Eucharist is the antidote to the human condition, the agent of transforming our human weakness into a living sacrifice offered for the salvation of souls. By it we are transformed into living Eucharist, radiating His mercy.

We can learn from St. Faustina how to draw all our strength from the Eucharist:

> One thing alone sustains me, and that is Holy Communion. From it I draw my strength; in it is all my comfort. ... Jesus concealed in the Host is everything to me. From the tabernacle I draw strength, power, courage and light. ... I would not know how to give glory to God if I did not have the Eucharist in my heart (1037).

What can you and I do to use the Eucharist as an antidote to our untransformed human condition and as a stepping stone to mature sanctity? We can make His offering of Mass the center of our lives:

> Taking part in the Eucharistic Sacrifice, which is the fount and apex of the whole Christian life, they (Christians) offer the divine victim to God, and offer themselves along with it (Vatican II, L.G. #11).

By Holy Orders the priest consecrates Eucharist, by

Holy Baptism we all offer the divine Victim and receive Him in Holy Communion. By offering and receiving the Immaculate Victim we are transformed.

We can continue our participation in this "miracle of mercy" (*Diary*, 1489) and come to this "fountain of mercy" (1817) in the following ways: by a spiritual offering of our sufferings and pains in union with the Eucharistic sacrifice; by our spiritual communions which we make with our hearts, welcoming and thanking Jesus; and by our adoration of the Blessed Sacrament present on the altar and in the tabernacle. We can take extended times of adoration as a regular part of our spiritual life. We need these times of silent presence to the One who is radiantly present. We need to open our hearts to "Radiation Therapy" which transforms our human condition!

As the bread and wine are transubstantiated into the Body and Blood of the Lord, so we, too, are to be transformed. After the consecration the priest invokes the Holy Spirit, that we may become the living Body of Christ:

> Grant that we, who are nourished by His body and blood, may be filled with His Holy Spirit, and become one body, one spirit in Christ (Third Eucharistic Prayer of the Roman Rite).

As we are transformed by the Eucharist into the living Body of Christ, we become more and more a countersign to our age: we begin to radiate His holiness as a countersign to the loss of the sense of sin; and we radiate His humility and His mercy as a countersign to a proud and self-centered generation.

GUILT

Being sinful, divided, unforgiving;
feeling unworthy, no-good,
bitter, despondent

RECONCILIATION

Being reconciled to God
by Confession and to one another
by mutual forgiveness.

CHAPTER NINE

SCRIPTURAL RESPONSE:

Nor do I condemn you. You may go. But from now on, avoid this sin (Jn 8:11).

Be reconciled to God! (2 Cor 5:21).

Be kind to one another, compassionate, and mutually forgiving, just as God has forgiven you in Christ (Eph 4:32).

RESPONSE FROM ST. FAUSTINA:

When you approach the confessional, know this, that I myself am waiting there for you. I am only hidden by the priest, but I myself act in your soul. Here the misery of the soul meets the God of mercy (*Diary*, 1602).

We come to confession to be healed; we come to be educated — like a small child, our soul has constant need of education (*Diary*, 377).

Tell souls that from this fount of mercy souls draw graces solely with the vessel of trust. If their trust is great, there is no limit to My generosity (*Diary*, 1602).

RECONCILIATION AS A
STEPPING STONE TO SANCTITY

St. Paul strongly implores us in the name of Christ: "Be reconciled to God!" (2 Cor 5:21) ... so that we may be ministers of reconciliation, ambassadors for Christ" (see 2 Cor 5:17-21). To be ministers of reconciliation we must first receive God's mercy and His forgiveness of our sins, so that we may forgive as we are forgiven (see Mt 6:12). You cannot give what you don't have. Having received mercy, we are to give mercy from the heart (see Mt. 18:35).

Reconciliation is so needed in our human condition! We are sinful, guilty, despondent, resentful, and divided, with deep feelings of unworthiness and shame.

Reconciliation lets mercy flow. We are reconciled to God and His Church by the Sacrament of Reconciliation, and to one another by mutual forgiveness.

In the Sacrament of Reconciliation the priest acts in the person of Christ and forgives the sins we bring. The priest prays in the name of God and the Church:

> God, the Father of mercies, through the death and resurrection of His Son, has reconciled the world to Himself and sent the Holy Spirit among us for the forgiveness of sins; through the ministry of the Church may God give you pardon and peace, and I absolve you from your sins in the name of the Father, and of the Son, and of the Holy Spirit. Amen.

What a miracle of mercy we have in this "Tribunal of Mercy" (*Diary*, 1448)! This is not a court of law dispensing justice and condemnation with others accusing us; rather, it is a court of mercy, where we accuse ourselves and have the Holy Spirit as our defense lawyer and Jesus as our judge dispensing mercy. Our Lord told St. Faustina:

> **Tell souls where they are to look for solace; that is, in the Tribunal of Mercy. There the greatest miracles take place [and] are incessantly repeated (1448).**

As ministers and ambassadors of reconciliation, we can forgive others seventy times seven every day (see Mt 18:22). We can "broadcast" forgiveness to those in need by praying "Jesus, Mercy" at every occasion that calls for reconciliation, forgiveness, and mercy. This business of praying "Jesus, Mercy" becomes a full-time job!

We can pray with great trust for sinners who are in the greatest need of mercy. Our Lord told St. Faustina:

> **The greater the sinner, the greater the right he has to My mercy (723). Pray for souls that they be not afraid to approach the tribunal of My mercy. Do not grow weary of praying for sinners (975).**

"Holy Mary, Mother of God, pray for us sinners now ... " All of us are sinners, and we are in solidarity with the sin of the world, so we all need prayer for mercy.

Through the whole celebration of Mass, the Church prays for mercy for the forgiveness of sin: in the opening penitential rite; in the solemn words of consecration; in the Lord's prayer; in the plea "Lamb of God, you take away the sins of the world: have mercy on us"; and in the prayer before receiving Holy Communion: "Lord, I am not worthy to receive you, but only say the word and I shall be healed."

The sin and division in the Church and world are so rampant, and the times are so urgent that we need God's mercy *now*! We need God's mercy to reconcile us to Himself, to His Church, and to one another.

Pope John Paul II, in his encyclical *Rich in Mercy* (#15), strongly urges us to appeal to God's mercy now. Our Lord's words to St. Faustina also stress the urgency of appealing to this mercy:

> **Mankind will not have peace until it turns with trust to My mercy (300). Speak to the world about My mercy; let all mankind recognize My unfathomable mercy. It is a sign for the end times; after it will come the day of justice. While there is still time, let them have recourse to the fount of My mercy; let them profit from the Blood and Water which gushed forth for them (848).**

Now is the time to be reconciled. Now is the time to receive God's mercy and be merciful. Now is the time to be forgiven and to forgive.

POWERLESSNESS

Being at a loss, powerless,
without purpose, without answers,
without faith, hope, or love.

PRAYER

Asking continuously for God's mercy
and the power of the Holy Spirit
for ourselves and others.

CHAPTER TEN

SCRIPTURAL RESPONSE:

Ask … seek … knock … How much more will the heavenly Father give the Holy Spirit to those who ask him (Lk 11:9-13).

RESPONSE FROM ST. FAUSTINA:

O my God, I am conscious of my mission in the Holy Church. It is my constant endeavor to plead for mercy for the world (*Diary*, 482).

The good God entrusted her [the sister of St. Faustina] to my care, and for two weeks I was able to work with her. But how many sacrifices this soul cost me is known only to God. For no other soul did I bring so many sacrifices and sufferings and prayers before the throne of God as I did for her soul. I felt that I had *forced God* to grant her grace. When I reflect on all this, I see that it was truly a miracle. *Now I can see how much power intercessory prayer has before God* (*Diary*, 202).

Jesus, I beg You, by the inconceivable power of Your mercy, that all the souls who will die today escape the fire of hell, even if they have been the greatest sinners. … Jesus pressed me to His Heart and said, **You have come to know well the depths of My mercy. *I will do what you ask*, but unite yourself continually with My agonizing Heart and make reparation to My justice** (*Diary*, 873).

PRAYER AS A STEPPING STONE TO SANCTITY

How can prayer be an antidote to our needs? Probably the simplest answer to this question is the command of Jesus. He simply said, "*ask.*" He went on to explain:

> Ask and you shall receive; seek and you shall find; knock and it shall be opened to you. For whoever asks, receives; whoever seeks, finds; whoever knocks, is admitted. ... How much more will the heavenly Father give the Holy Spirit to those who ask Him (Lk 11:9-13).

And in our human condition we have intense needs — so many people are powerless, without purpose, without answers and, most importantly, without faith, hope, or love. The greatest need is for God's mercy, mercy that brings His forgiveness, His reconciliation, His salvation, His love. Only the Holy Spirit, the Spirit of Mercy, the giver of all "good things" (as described in Mt 7:11) can answer our real needs.

But our receiving God's mercy depends on our freely asking for it, because God so respects our freedom that He will not violate it. He waits for us to exercise our freedom by asking with trust for what we need. When we do this, we give God the freedom to act! By prayer we give God permission to be merciful to us. And His mercy far exceeds our needs and our asking. His mercy is greater than our plans. So when we pray, we allow God to fulfill His plan, in His way, and in His timing. And His plan is to have mercy on all (see Rom 11:32).

St. Faustina's life was dedicated to prayer, and she constantly asked for God's mercy for those in need. One of the prayers the Lord taught her to use was the Chaplet of Divine Mercy, which He told her to say unceasingly (474). Awed by the effectiveness of this prayer, she wrote, "Never before had I prayed with such inner power" (474).

The text of the Chaplet of Divine Mercy is a Eucharistic offering. It echoes the prayer of St. Michael at Fatima, and is like a "mini-Mass" that we can repeat throughout the day:

> Eternal Father, I offer You the Body and Blood, Soul and Divinity of Your dearly beloved Son, Our Lord Jesus Christ, in atonement for our sins and those of the whole world; for the sake of His sorrowful Passion, have mercy on us and on the whole world (476).

An even shorter form of asking for God's mercy is the simple exclamation, "Jesus, Mercy!" We cry out with our hearts, even as St. Faustina did, to Jesus, whose Heart was opened for us as the fountain of the Father's mercy. By this prayer we not only honor Jesus as Divine Mercy Itself; but we also ask Him to have mercy on us, on our present need, on the Church and on the whole world. "Jesus, Mercy" can be a continual cry of our heart and our lips as we encounter the needs of the human condition. "Jesus, Mercy" is a mini-Chaplet, just as the Chaplet is a mini-Mass.

Praying for God's mercy is also a stepping stone to sanctity. When we ask for mercy, we also ask for and receive the Holy Spirit, the Spirit of Mercy. It is the Holy Spirit who transforms us, who is poured into our hearts (see Rom 5:5) and makes us holy. The Holy Spirit transforms our earthen vessels, all our misery, into His temples! Holiness is not so much the vessel as the content within the vessel; that is, the living presence of the Holy Spirit.

The more we ask for God's mercy, the more we are transformed into vessels of that mercy to a world in need. And there is no doubt that the world's greatest need is God's mercy — *now*!

This urgency is one of the major messages of Our Lord to St. Faustina, a message for the whole world:

> **Speak to the world about My mercy; let all mankind recognize My unfathomable mercy. It is a sign for the end times; after it will come the day of justice. While there is still time, let them have recourse to the fount of My mercy; let them profit from the Blood and Water which gushed forth for them (848).**

BURN-OUT

Feeling persecuted,
confused, tormented, distressed,
tired, lonely, lost, trapped.

THE MERCIFUL HEART
OF JESUS

Resting in the
Heart of Jesus, seeking to
unite our hearts to His.

CHAPTER ELEVEN

SCRIPTURAL RESPONSE:

Come to me, all you who are weary and find life burdensome (Mt 11:28-29).

"Put your hand into my side ... and believe!" (Jn 20:27).

RESPONSE FROM ST. FAUSTINA:

My daughter, know that My Heart is mercy itself. ... No soul that has approached Me has ever gone away unconsoled. All misery gets buried in the depths of My mercy (*Diary*, 1777).

When I see that the burden is beyond my strength, I do not consider or analyze it or probe into it, but I run like a child to the Heart of Jesus and say only one word to Him: "You can do all things." And then I keep silent ... (*Diary*, 1033, see also 1621, 1629).

THE MERCIFUL HEART AS A STEPPING STONE TO SANCTITY

If you are being attacked or persecuted, even by friends; if you are tormented, distressed, confused, fearful, tired out, burned out, weak, lonely, or just lost; then you need the refuge and rest that can only be found in the Merciful Heart of Jesus. Even if you can check off only one of the above, the antidote is still the same. The Merciful Heart of Jesus was opened up on the cross as a source of mercy, and as a stronghold for us in our attacked human condition.

The Lord taught St. Faustina to pattern her whole life on His Heart:

> **My daughter, I desire that your heart be formed after the model of My merciful Heart. You must be completely imbued with My mercy"** (167).

He made it clear to her that her life and mission had to be based on the union of her heart with His:

> **My spouse, our hearts are joined forever"** (239).

Out of this union of hearts would flow His mercy:

> **My daughter, I desire that your heart be an abiding place of My mercy. I desire**

that this mercy flow out upon the whole world through your heart" (1777).

The most obvious characteristic of the life of St. Faustina was her intimacy with the Lord. This intimacy, this union of hearts, was the foundation of both her spiritual life and her mission as the secretary and apostle of Divine Mercy. On every page of her diary, we see examples of this intimate union with God — how she loved Him, suffered with Him, talked to Him, prayed to Him. Her whole life was preoccupied and possessed by God, who loved her with His tender mercy. She was often invited by the Lord to rest on His Heart like the beloved disciple (*Diary*, 801, 929, 1348).

This intimate union with the Merciful Heart of Jesus is extended to us by the Lord Himself: "Come to me, all you who are weary and find life burdensome, and I will refresh you. Take my yoke upon your shoulders and learn from me, for I am gentle and humble of heart. Your souls will find rest, for My yoke is easy and my burden light" (Mt 11:28-30).

Like St. Faustina, we can surrender our hearts to the Merciful Heart of Jesus by our *trust* in Him, and thus, we, too, can live in an intimate union with Him. This is the Lord's desire and invitation. This is why His Heart was pierced for us on the Cross as a fount of mercy. St. John, as an eyewitness to the piercing of the side of Jesus, tells us that it was done as a final sign so that we would look upon Him whom they have pierced and *believe* — believe with a committed faith (Jn 19:33-37).

And so we are to cry out with the great cry of trust of Thomas when he saw the pierced side and put his hand into the wound: "My Lord and My God!" (Jn 20:28).

We, too, like St. Faustina, are to rest on the Heart of Jesus, to live in the Lord, who is present to our hearts by the gift of the Holy Spirit (see Rom 5:5). What a merciful God we have, that He should be present to us in our human condition! When we are present to the Lord with our hearts, in the Heart of Our Mother Mary, trusting and rejoicing, we can live in continual prayer, in continual intimacy with the Lord who loves us.

This intimacy of hearts with the Lord is a gift that is available for the asking! Each of us can ask, "Lord change my heart. Make my heart like yours. Lord, draw me, that I may be drawn. Fill me with the fire of your divine love. Fill me with your mercy, that I may radiate your mercy to others. Come, Holy Spirit. Come, Lord Jesus!"

The Merciful Heart of Jesus is not only an antidote to our attacked human condition; it is *the* great stepping stone to sanctity, to our intimate union with God. In the Merciful Heart of Jesus we learn and experience that God is Mercy Itself, that He is all in all, the first always and everywhere, the beginning and the end. He is the fire that enkindles our hearts with a living flame and transforms us (*Diary*, 1050, 1140) so that "[it] is no longer I who live, but Christ who lives in me" (Gal 2:20 RSV).

The intimate union of our hearts with the Heart of Jesus means that we live in complete surrender to Him, seeking only Him. This is why He created us free, so that we may love Him and serve Him with our whole hearts — freely. This is why He permits us to fall in our human condition, so that we might turn to Him with our whole hearts and receive His mercy. What He asks of all of us is to *trust Him*, so that He may be merciful to all (Rom 11:32).

INSECURITY

Feeling helpless, confused,
sad, sorry for self,
unsure of self.

MOTHER OF MERCY

Accepting the mother of
Jesus as our mother, too, allowing
her to comfort and form us.

SCRIPTURAL RESPONSE:

Behold your mother! (Jn 19:27).

Do whatever he tells you (Jn 2:5).

Come children, hear me; I will teach you the fear of the Lord (Ps 34:12).

RESPONSE FROM ST. FAUSTINA:

My daughter, at God's command I am to be, in a special and exclusive way, your Mother; but I desire that you, too, in a special way be my child (Diary, 1414).

My daughter, what I demand from you is prayer, prayer, and once again prayer, for the world and especially for your country (Diary, 325).

She [the Mother of God] has taught me how to love God interiorly and also how to carry out His holy will in all things (*Diary*, 40).

O Mary, my Mother and my Lady, I offer you my soul, my body, my life and my death, and all that will follow it. I place everything in your hands (*Diary*, 79).

The Mother of God told me to do what She had done, that, even when joyful, I should always keep my eyes fixed on the cross (*Diary*, 561).

THE MOTHER OF MERCY AS A STEPPING STONE TO SANCTITY

Mary is the Mother of Jesus and our mother. As His dying gesture of mercy on the cross, Jesus gave us His mother to be our own mother. He spoke to all of us when he said to the beloved disciple: "Behold, your Mother!" (Jn 19:27 NABR).

Our Blessed Mother told Faustina:

> I am not only the Queen of Heaven, but also the Mother of Mercy and your Mother" (330). "I am Mother to you all, thanks to the unfathomable mercy of God" (449).

The Second Vatican Council teaches us that Mary, as the Mother of God, cares for us:

> She is a mother to us in the order of grace ... for, taken up to heaven, she did not lay aside this saving role, but by her manifold acts of intercession continues to win for us gifts of eternal salvation. By her maternal charity, Mary cares for the brethren of her son (*Lumen Gentium*, 61-62).

As our heavenly Mother, Mary is the antidote to our insecurity, the Mother of Mercy who, by her "maternal charity," helps us when we are helpless, confused, sorry for ourselves, sad, depressed, lonely, or lustful.

Yes, she can help us, because the Lord has chosen her to be an integral part of our redemption. The Father chose Mary to be the Mother of His Son by the power of the Holy Spirit. Since God chose her, she is no longer an option on our part. Mary is ever Mother. She is a powerful and necessary intercessor and mediator because of God's choice and plan. She carries out God's plan by the power of the Holy Spirit, her spouse. As Mother she continues to form us by the Spirit to be like Jesus. We go to Jesus the way He came to us — through Mary.

Anticipating the victory of the cross, Mary, conceived Immaculate in the womb of Anne, longs to share her special graces with her children — even the grace of her "Immaculateness." St. Faustina, after persistently asking it of Mary for many years, received the gift of purity, and was never again subject to temptations against it (see *Diary*, 40).

As the Mother of Mercy, Mary forms us, nurtures us, teaches us, guides, and protects us. She can point to herself as the model of mercy and trust. And we can trust her because, as Pope John Paul II tells us, she is the "mediatrix of mercy" (*Mother of the Redeemer* #41).

Like St. Faustina, we, too, can be "special" children of Mary (*Diary*, 240, 1414). How? By *asking* for what we need and by *entrusting* our lives to Mary so that she may form us into the living image of Jesus. By entrusting our lives to Mary, we give her permission to act freely and bring us to the pierced Heart of Jesus on the cross, the source of all mercy. This is the meaning of consecration to Jesus through Mary. At the cross, by the radiance of His Blood and water, we are transformed. We become living Eucharist and radiate His mercy. From Mary, we can learn to live the *Magnificat*, glorifying God, rejoicing in His mercy, and proclaiming it to every generation (see Lk 1:50).

One form of consecration to our Mother of Mercy is based on John 19:25-27. We can use it daily, asking Mary to be Our Mother and to form us as she formed Jesus by the Spirit:

An Act of Consecration to Mary

Mary, Mother of Jesus
and Mother of Mercy,
since Jesus from the Cross gave you to me,
I take you as my own.
And since Jesus gave me to you,
take me as your own.
Make me docile like Jesus on the Cross,
obedient to the Father,
trusting in humility and in love.
Mary, my Mother,
in imitation of the Father,
who gave His Son to you,
I too give my all to you;
to you I entrust all that I am,
all that I have and all that I do.
Help me to surrender
ever more fully to the Spirit.
Lead me deeper into the Mystery
of the Cross, the Cenacle
and the fullness of Church.
As you formed the heart of Jesus by the Spirit,
form my heart to be the throne of Jesus
in His glorious coming.

AFTERWORD

What is the bottom line of the twelve antidotes and stepping stones? What does it all mean? What is the goal we should be trying to achieve?

The ultimate goal of all of our lives should be the **union of hearts**, the intimate union of our hearts with the Merciful Heart of Jesus by the transformation of His mercy. As the Holy Spirit is poured into our hearts, we are transformed into living Eucharist, and thus radiate His mercy to a world so much in need.

The very misery of our human condition is transformed by the Spirit of Mercy into something holy. It is like the Spirit of God that hovered over the chaos in creation (see Gen 1:2) and brought forth light and life. The Holy Spirit hovers over our chaos to bring forth eternal light and life — the new creation. The Holy Spirit, the Spirit of Mercy, is the active agent of our sanctification. As Jesus offered Himself up through the Eternal Spirit (see Heb 9:14) and sanctified our suffering and misery into sacrifice bringing us salvation, so we, too, offer up our human condition through the Eternal Spirit to be transformed and sanctified, to become living Eucharist.

By the Holy Spirit we are divinized, made members of the Body of Christ. It is a transformation that St. Faustina experienced and described in various ways. When she made the free oblation of herself and all her sufferings for souls, especially sinners, she experienced what she described as being "transconsecrated" (*Diary*, 137). She prayed often to become a "living host" (*Diary*, 642, 832, 1289, 1392, 1564, 1622, 1826), a small wafer, hidden and given in love, completely transformed into His mercy (*Diary*, 514, 692).

How can we become apostles of Divine Mercy like St. Faustina? By living the twelve characteristic features of her spiritual life and mission, and by living the Sacred Scriptures as she did. She didn't write commentaries on the Word of God, but she was a living model of that Word.

In the Letter to the Hebrews, for example, we can see the scriptural foundation of the spirituality and mission of Divine Mercy recorded in the *Diary* of St. Faustina. The author of the letter describes Jesus as the trustworthy and merciful High Priest, who identified Himself with His brethren in His passion, becoming victim and priest, offering Himself through the Eternal Spirit for the salvation of all. So by His mercy He was "perfected," or transformed, and declared High Priest — in perfect relationship with God and mankind. He became the source of mercy for all who come to Him.

St. Faustina trusted in the merciful High Priest and totally identified with Him as victim, becoming a channel of His mercy to all in need. We, too, are invited to trust in Jesus, the merciful High Priest, and unite with Him as victims of mercy for souls. Like Jesus and Mary, and like St. Faustina, we are called to humble obedience to the will of God.

As apostles of Divine Mercy, we, too, are to *obtain* and *proclaim* God's mercy as St. Faustina did (see *Diary*, 436), and so glorify the Divine Mercy as the very reason and purpose of our lives (see *Diary*, 1242).

Another way to live the message and mission of Divine Mercy is to fulfill the exhortations of St. Paul to the

Thessalonians. St. Faustina did not comment on this text of the word of God, but she obviously heard it and acted upon it:

> *Rejoice* always, *pray* without ceasing, in all things give *thanks,* for this is the *will of God in Christ Jesus* regarding *you all* (1 Thess 5:16-18, Confraternity edition).

St. Faustina did, indeed, *"rejoice* always." The main witnesses to this are the sworn testimonies of the sisters who lived with her (testimonies of witnesses for her beatification process). They were amazed how joyful she was in the midst of hard work and sickness.

To "*pray* without ceasing" was the mission of her life (*Diary,* 482). Mary taught her the importance of praying always: *"My daughter, what I demand of you is prayer, prayer, and once again prayer"* (*Diary,* 325). She prayed for sinners, priests, souls in purgatory. Our Lord directed her: **"Say unceasingly the chaplet that I taught you"** (*Diary,* 687).

"In all things give *thanks"* was expressed in the Eucharistic thanksgiving which was the center of St. Faustina's life. She especially gave thanks in suffering for souls (see *Diary,* 343) and in the humiliations of her daily life (*Diary,* 92, 593).

"The *will of God"* was what St. Faustina sought with her whole will and life (*Diary,* 374, 821, 652, 724, 821, 952). She completely united her will to His.

"*In Christ Jesus"* — this was the foundation of her Apostolate of Divine Mercy, to be in union with the Merciful Heart of Jesus.

"Regarding *you all"* — St. Faustina was told that what

she wrote about the message of Divine Mercy was for all the souls throughout the world who would seek Him.

To live the word of *rejoicing, praying, thanking* always *in Christ Jesus*, is to trust the Merciful Savior and to live in union with Him, proclaiming and glorifying His mercy, like Mary, Our Mother; and like our sister, St. Faustina, the secretary and apostle of Divine Mercy. It is to live the glorious Magnificat of Mary, to radiate His mercy as living Eucharist, to be an apostle of Divine Mercy.

A Consecration to the Sacred
and Merciful Heart of Jesus

Lord Jesus, You invite me to come to You.
So I come to Your Sacred and Merciful Heart,
the fountain of all mercy,
with my sins, my misery, and my burdens.
Cleanse me, transform me,
and fill me with Your mercy.

Jesus, You invite me to take Your yoke.
So I take up my daily cross,
to walk in trust, in step with You.
I offer You my whole self as a living sacrifice.
Make me holy and acceptable to the Father
and make my heart like Yours.
As Your Heart was pierced for me,
pierce my heart to be a channel of mercy for others.

Jesus, You invite me to learn from You.
So teach me Your gentleness and humility.
As a child dependent on Your mercy,
I take refuge in Your Heart.
I want to do Your will and glorify Your mercy.

Jesus, You promised to refresh me.
So let me find peace
by resting on Your Heart like John.
I want to be present to You with my heart,
and radiate your presence to others.

By Rev. George W. Kosicki, C.S.B. © 1993, Marian Helpers

ABOUT THE AUTHOR

Known and loved throughout the world, Fr. Kosicki is truly a spiritual father, blessing people just by his presence, bringing light and joy to all wherever he goes. His popular talks about Divine Mercy are a unique blend of strong teaching, spontaneous song, light-hearted anecdotes, and deep spirituality. And, with a doctorate in biochemistry, Fr. Kosicki may also tickle your mind with a little "scientific formula" now and then to emphasize a special spiritual concept.

But above all, Fr. Kosicki is a man of prayer. Fueled by three hours a day in front of the Blessed Sacrament, he is incredibly productive. He has been an active leader in the Charismatic renewal for thirty years, has spread devotion to Divine Mercy and to Our Lady through hundreds of retreats all over the world, and has hosted several TV series. In addition to his twenty-four research publications in biochemistry, he has produced several hundred articles, audio and video tapes, books and booklets — including a dozen books on Divine Mercy.

Spiritual director for Spirit Song Ministries, Fr. Kosicki is currently pursuing a hermit's life of prayer and writing in the wilderness of Michigan's Upper Peninsula.

Other Books by
Fr. George Kosicki, C.S.B.

Spiritual Warfare: Attack Against the Woman

Does Satan really exist? Are there really evil spirits? Many in our contemporary society say, "No." In this book you'll find out how wrong they are. St. Paul wasn't kidding when he warned us that we're fighting more than just flesh and blood and that we need to arm ourselves for the battle (Eph 6:12). Now in its second printing, *Spiritual Warfare* gives clear answers and straightforward facts to help you understand the plan and tactics of the enemy and learn how best to defend yourself and your loved ones. 146 pages. ISBN: 0-9625975-4-6. $6.00

Rejoice in the Lord Always!

Of all the books Fr. Kosicki has written, *Rejoice* is his favorite. It's a book he, himself, has to reread at least once a year, "because I need it." Written in a simple, conversational style, *Rejoice* flows from the heart of a man known and loved around the world for his ability to bless and bring joy to those around him. We all need to read and reread it, to discover what Christian joy really is and learn how to make it an integral part of our lives. 92 pages. ISBN: 0-944203-18-3. $8.00

Other Books by
Fr. George Kosicki, C.S.B.

Now is the Time for Mercy

Written with Vinny Flynn in response to the need for a complete handbook to the Divine Mercy message and devotion, *Now is the Time for Mercy* has become the most popular book about Divine Mercy. You'll find clear, complete explanations of the message of mercy from the Diary of St. Faustina, with detailed discussions of the Divine Mercy Image, the Chaplet, the Novena, the Feast, the Hour of Mercy, and how to become an apostle of Mercy like St. Faustina. 104 pages. **ISBN: 0-944203-05-1. $8.00**

Intercession: Moving Mountains Eucharistically

As coordinator of the Bethany House of Intercession for nine years, Fr. Kosicki gained a wealth of experience about the power of intercessory prayer — especially when linked to a Eucharistic way of life. Now he shares that experience with you. Here you'll learn how to "intercede at the intersections" of your life, bring new power to your prayer, begin to live Eucharistically, and find real value and meaning even in the inevitable sufferings that come your way. You, too, can move mountains! 95 pages. **ISBN: 1-880033-20-8. $5.00**

Spirit Song Ministries is a recording/publishing company established in 1993 by Vinny and Donna Flynn to produce and distribute their family music albums, talks on tape, and religious publications.

It is now a full-time family apostolate, whose offerings include: The Chaplet of Divine Mercy (sung in English or Spanish); Still Waters music albums; contemporary praise and worship albums; Christmas music; Catholic Teachings on Tape, and inspirational books.

For a complete catalog, write or call:

Spirit Song Ministries
60 Interlaken Road, P.O. Box 486
Stockbridge, MA 01262-0486
Tel. 413-298-3105 Fax 413-298-4065
Toll Free 1-888-549-8009